AF326567

SELECTED POEMS

Nancy Anne Miller

Selected Poems

VP

Valley Press

First published in 2024 by Valley Press
Woodend, The Crescent, Scarborough, UK, YO11 2PW
valleypressuk.com

ISBN 978-1-915606-48-8
Cat. no. VP0239

Copyright © Nancy Anne Miller 2024

The right of Nancy Anne Miller to be identified as the
author of this work has been asserted in accordance with
the Copyright, Designs and Patents Act 1988.

All rights reserved. No part of this publication may be
reproduced, stored in or introduced into a retrieval system,
or transmitted in any form, by any means (electronic,
mechanical, photocopying, recording or otherwise) without
prior written permission from the rights holders.

Cover and text design by Jamie McGarry.
Cover illustration by Jane Morse.

Contents

for
Mary Diana Hutchings

*"I wish that I could find an event that
meant as much as simply seeing."*
Theodore Roethke, Poet

*"But how can this thing be made so that you can catch the
mystery of appearance within the mystery of the making?"*
Francis Bacon, Painter

CONCH

Conch

The ocean makes a sculpture of turning:
carves the spiral, the journey of sound into ear.

The line of the tide's deep roar, white-tipped
as the lip of a wave: the sea's mouth foams.

Pearl

The sun's steering wheel
turns the large house,
inside, photographs radiate light,
link into a string of pearls.

'Pearl', the family ship,
sank during the nineteenth century,
shed a cargo of onions
to bead the ocean floor.

Women's mouths are sealed
into the thin edges of an oyster
wearing a choker of pearls.
A necklace of small restful

moons shines out under
hushed voiced waves,
when a woman does not plunge
into her own stormy depths.

Banana Bunch

A catcher's mitt
stops the fast
ball sun. A fat

woman's glove,
seams split,
her hand turns

to sugar. One
banana is
the moon's finger,

draws every-
thing into
a circular whole.

Devonshire Moon

Cows sound
its name
during the day
moo moo moo

Milk white
surrounds
their shadows
at night

It takes eating
the earth all day
to prevent
their flying to it

Tea Service

The silver teapot sails
the mahogany table. A dark Indian
Ocean ripples the afternoon's sheen.

The creamer prams milk
from the cows of the home-hills,
the dairy-fresh landscapes.

Sugar stacks up
the way an empire is built,
raw brown whitened into cubes.

SOMERSAULT

Navel String

Bermudians do not follow the Caribbean custom
of burying umbilical cords in their backyard.

A dried twine of glue which holds a soul
to a birthplace. That is not how I'm pulled back.

Rather, I wake in the middle of the night to bring
the hibiscus plants in because the temperature has

dropped, each bud folded like a bird asleep.
"You are a sixteenth-generation Bermudian,"

cousin Lisa would say. I carry them in like any
immigrant who brings a bush from home to grow,

but these will never settle in New England dirt.
I must wait until the end of May to re-pot them,

slip tight new shoes on their feet where roots will
not spread, warm as toes in sand. I must wait until

the weekend Bermudians celebrate the Queen's
birthday by taking a swim. We then plant

ourselves firmly between the waves' furrows. Their
buoyant line, a tugging navel string, anchors us.

Somersault

It must be that we are drawn
back to the ocean, because waves
rise like days in their own definition
before becoming flat, one with sea.

I'm sure it is how we remember
a specific moment, before it curls
into all times, or becomes scattered
as a net of spray pulling in the new.

Or, is it because we drifted into
the world, feet fin-like, practicing
the somersaults we will do to keep
afloat, but with a safety rope still intact.

Jellyfish

The odd lace sleeve floats
off a dress. A slip from
down under, the ocean's
soft filmy lingerie.

A watery mouth whispers
words that the sea forms
and un-forms, the un-said
depth of currents and tides.

So defenceless that only
a sting could guard
this transparent being,
a red line leaves a mark.

Like badminton shuttlecocks
bouncing on the wave's net;
un-aimed, un-intended,
they float by me.

I dodge them in the surf;
don't want to disturb this
layered formlessness, want
to let a see-through life just live.

Ear Drum

The woman pushing the shopping cart
with a crumpled plastic white bag inside,
like a discarded embryo or an ear,
could have been my Bermudian maid

who, when strolling me in my pram,
muttered, "Ugly dark woman!"
as we passed a Jamaican on the road.
How could I know of such differences,

except in voice rhythms in the air;
the deeply quiet Bermudian tone,
and the melodic sing-song West Indian?
Like the waves formed their dialect,

and ours, smooth as a rock, was worn down
from the lapping tide. Bermuda had
to stay solid, steady, so alone,
almost seven hundred miles out at sea.

I lay in a Liberty of London dress,
a smocked garden of English flowers,
shook a silver rattler, back and forth,
back and forth, joined in with a petite maraca.

Elephant Horn

A husk taken from a 'long-
memoried' beast, the ivory
horn warned of slavers nearby.
Hard to forget a trade treating

humans like animals, linked
to one another in a parading circus.
My teapot lifts its spout up,
a blaring trunk. East India leaves,

steep, brackish as shadows.
Bermuda's Elephant Plant spreads
wide green ears, large enough
to hear what cries out in the bush.

A History of Knives

The police woman sits
with a large knife in her hand.
On the mat in front of her are
machetes, hatchets and scythes.

She looks like any maid who
cleans the kitchen cutlery,
displays them on the dining
table and inspects one to see

if it is sharp enough to glide
through a tender leg of lamb
for a Sunday dinner. Where
outside her gardener husband

might fell the fennel with
the rhythm and swoosh of
lapping waves, as a green wake
follows his swashbuckling path.

The cook would chop, chop,
bananas, paw, paw, peppers,
a collage of bright colour
she made for the daily meal.

Now her great-grandsons use tools
meant for outside work,
to slice a bag off a tourist's shoulder
like a heavy and ripe mango.

When her ancestors crossed the Atlantic,
chained as meat in a butcher's
locker, they tried to find any sharp
instrument to cut themselves free.

Post-Colonial Pie

There was no mother in the kitchen
pressing out pastry on the long conveyor belt
of women rolling out pies
for family, friends, the community.

No mother to gather apples from an orchard,
fill an apron with the earth's fruit,
hand clasped to her belly to hold the bulging cargo,
that might spill over the ground, a woman pregnant

with the season's bounty. Just Nedra,
late for work after a night of men, cards,
dancing and booze, hickeys all over her neck,
leeches sucking up the last bits of love.

Nedra with the rolling pin held the way
an English Bobby holds his baton,
retrieving bits of flour and butter,
islands she pressed into one whole piece,

a woman mending a map. Nedra, who
spiked the pie with rum, mangoes, loquats,
cinnamon, cloves. The pie, a ship bearing
her African ancestors' flavours.

Her slave bracelets rattling as she pressed
down the pastry, an oarswoman
smoothing out a wave. My own pies
do not poof up in New England fashion,

edges flounced like a curtain ruffled in a breeze.
My crusts are handkerchiefs, rags wrapped
around what a hand grabs up in a hurry to smuggle
across the border of one country into the next.

Ebury Court Hotel

Thank God I'm not at the Ebury
on a rainy day in London,
when the parlour's bottom window
is a glass half empty not full.

When the flowered chintz on the couch
has faded into veins on an old body,
and the Country Life magazines curl
at the edges like a dog's docked tail.

Thank God I'm not there when
the radiators hiss like an elderly woman,
sighing in her arthritic bones,
after riding her mare through the park.

Better to be there when daffodils
brighten the green with their yellows,
like miniatures of the sun up close,
usually too polite to ever be seen.

BECAUSE THERE WAS NO SEA

Nothing

Nothing grows in a straight line here.
Oleander boughs curl, wriggle flowers
like painted pink toes for tourists.

Cacti flail thorny branches over walls,
octopi renege the nearby presence
of a gadabout summer swimmer.

Standard English won't grow vertical,
in the Stonehenge temple of teeth.
Drops an octave, swoons like sea grass

in a tide. Scatters tongues on the beach
in shells, tell of the in, out of ocean,
tiny scallop shovels which dig deep.

I turn brown as the earth below me,
my accent a thick shade, skin peels,
a need to be dressed, undressed by sun.

Phone Cord

The phone may as well be a small pillow
we rest our head on. One from the nursery
where our wooden horse Doblin rocked

us like waves. It may as well be a conch
from off the beach where the echoes
of the ocean carry us, connect us to home.

The sound of water coming in and out
as voice patterns rise in a high tide or ebb
as we speak amongst ourselves: talk Bermudian.

The sea's slow surge is a hand kneading
my past, my present into one rhythm
which resides in my family's news trailing

through the phone cord, binds us
together. A long slack skipping rope
we twirl while each one takes their turn.

Because There Was No Sea

I took to sidewalk surfboarding the hills,
the blur of the landscape like
two gigantic waves on each side.

I stood outside in any downpour,
until my pockets filled out into
teats sloppy with water, water.

I cupped hands under blue hydrangeas,
bursting over picket fences in June
like fire hydrants in inner cities.

Stood in the shallow river rushing
underfoot, an escalator I could
ride, slide back down into the ocean.

Thin, cool, a silver shoehorn
slipping my sole into a fit cast
and made by tracks on pink beaches.

Sea Sick

Not what you think, not
experiencing the horizon
line seesawing while I
try to maintain a balance,
to make the world flat.

Rather, I smell the sea in
the Clorox-washed floor.
The seaweed stench of low
tide; strands embedded in
the beach like worms coiling.

The rot of wood on a punt,
so infested with the ocean
it smells of urine. Each
breaking wave, a haunch
lifted by a dog to own.

Airport Necklace

Made of small speckled beige shells,
one can imagine each snail came out
like a parachute or an airbag in a car.

Coil as a child's hand tightly holds
beach sand. I proudly wear the necklace
back from Tortola as if displaying a set

of lover's teeth. Think of the intimacy
of once cleaving to plants, slimy as
tears sticking. Empty now as slothful

inhabitants moved out. Curve with
a ram's horn scroll, announce
the crawl space of what is left behind.

The Sunday Times

The Phoenix Clock rises from
Queen Street in a steely white
Victorian elegance. We peer into it
as if it is a large magnifying glass
to study the contents of time. I wait

under the Guyanese Rubber Tree
until half four when the chemist
opens. Gangly limbs extend over
a spearheaded fence; jungle natives
hold a large beast at bay. I come

to Hamilton every Sunday with
father to pick up papers from
New York City brought in by
an afternoon flight, his homing
pigeon bearing news. He is eager

to view a world made black and
white as the T.V. we are one of
the first families to own. I grab
funnies, the only bit of colour
folded inside, bright as the island

we move through, window framed
by our car in comic strip sequence,
where figures are caught in a box like
ones pasted on large billboards, I
later drive by on American highways.

Blue Blood

White as the fresh meat of the Pompano, Bream,
Jacks which swam turquoise waters then were
displayed at Miles Market lying on cubes of ice,
scaled and up for sale. Jeremy Gorham's legs
above cashmere socks, below flannel pants
still worn in August, were pale, never brown,
blue English blood chilled his nine-year-old body.
He dragged the home country around in
his lungs, sacks of cold blowing across Devon.
When his face freckled, it smarted into gnat bites,
as if prickly heat stung cheeks red. Never
much at school, bookish, a collector of stamps,
he favoured lands filled with the sun: Africa,
India, the British Caribbean. His stacked Manila
envelopes golden as a tan he never had. His Gothic
home more grey, forlorn among Bermudian
pastel houses. Spires jutted up, the tips of bat wings.

Practice

The chicken wire over the glass
makes the gate mirrors crack,
put up to block balls while you
practice golf swings. Your club is
a quarter note driven by rhythm.

We collect them in a basket, look
for rubber eggs. Joke Portuguese
gardeners may mistake Dunhills
for potatoes. Their hoes strike soil
with enough force to attach them.

You place a small waterlogged moon
on a tee. Tack a spot on the island
map. Hit it like a semibreve into
the staff of phone lines. A score
sky writes about the vastness of blue.

Olivetti

If I could line letters up
like soldiers, the way they
are assembled in my Olivetti
typewriter with white shiny

cadet hats, I would. If I could
neaten the process of writing,
make it precise, orderly,
ceremonial, I would. Silver

rungs rise up, salute
each letter as they
march onto the page. If
I could make my writing

not skip a beat, and turn
back to form a new line
of thought at the sound
of a bell while I throw

the carrier back, like a private
changing a gun's position
from her left to right
shoulder, I would, if I could.

IMMIGRANT'S AUTUMN

We Did Not Know Yet

We didn't know yet that
we were immigrants too,
as we watched *West Side Story*
when we first came to America.

We didn't know how we would
miss our island as Jets hung
off fire escapes, colourful as
island lizards clinging to a stalk.

Jackknifing into whatever
emergency position the slums
required, like a Boy Scout's tool
for survival. We did not know as

we sat in tartan kilts, Shetland sweaters,
stayed at The Plaza, how we would
miss the fauna as their girlfriends
twirled in skirts the pink of hibiscus,

that our hearts would storm for
territory, be at war with America,
reject a romantic union with
the new world. A part of us would

die like the hero, his wound
blood-bright as a poppy we sold
on Front St. for Armistice Day
to honour whom did not surrender.

This is Not Your Ticket

Although as I print it out,
waves of white paper, surf,
rise out of the printer, curl,

part in the back, before falling
to the floor: the wake
of the ferry I will ride.

Remember as a child I thought
it meant 'fairy' an adult was
trying to catch, fool with

their shillings, like money
left under my pillow
for a tooth. The sight of

the two boats on the web,
noses almost touching,
dolphins, transports me

like a wand to ride one across
Hamilton Harbour, read
the Mid Ocean News tides schedule,

think they rose, fell by the weight,
and the amount of ships, freighters,
yachts, punts afloat on top of them.

Lionfish

Like it has been shocked from
the venom it carries on tips
of scales, the gold lines
vibrate in the water. Each jag-

ged stripe lightning in the sea.
A mouth large enough for
any shoplifter to have a day,
tosses butterfish, minnows

in like jewels. Floats above
reefs: an English sunset
over an expanding king-
dom from the Florida Keys

throughout the Caribbean.
MGM lion symbol for
the watery film of the deep,
it rewrites the reef's scripts.

Released from a private
aquarium into the vast
ocean, bright pieces of gold
fell from a silk purse. Won't

convert into local currency,
shakes up the underworld's
balance and turns up every-
where just like a bad penny.

Jump Rope on Court Street

The rope that bound ancestors,
frees as her heart pumps strong,
the curved line, the shape of
a cardiogram on a doctor's wall.

Not a hamster in a cage, she
skips with delight as the cord
strikes ground, a wave hits
shore after rising high behind her.

A wing flutters about her
as feet point, a ballerina
about to lift up, she holds
two propellers on both sides.

Like a dark iris inside an
eye which constantly blinks,
she sees so clearly the need
to be nimble, limber, jump high.

Salinas

I rake the bleached, washed ½ inch gravel I ordered
for my driveway; rake it like the slaves of ancestors
raked salt in the Salinas in Turks, Caicos, as if raking
whiteness out of the ocean, what belonged to a few.

I call it my beach in New England, the glare welcomes
as I make footprints into it, back and forth to my Saab.
The hibiscus planted in the urns will sun their chins
over it, feel the sub-tropical heat waves rise up. Such

simple things make a home. A Mediterranean
shimmer is a carpet transporting, a bridge to
warmth that will slosh up, into windowpanes
arranged like bar glasses to catch it, quench a thirst.

Lighthouse Keeping

Gibbs Hill Lighthouse
spills white light like
a saltshaker, pours sodium
into the air and ocean,

spreads it over the South
Shore, stiffens waves
into starched sheets, tips
peg them on a line.

I hear town trucks shovel
snow in CT, slam in
and out of my driveway,
a tide pounds with rhythm.

A permanent line of
breaking surf is left,
salt is being thrown
over the backs of fences.

I spread bits of sodium
in front of my saltbox
to melt a frozen path. Tears
that turn ice into saltwater.

Cruel Work 1900

She pricks the surface
of the cloth with the steel tip,
thin beak of a hummingbird
feeds on flowers, loops
of thread in constant motion,
invisible as helicopter wings.

A tattoo artist's skill to
imprint a patterned flower
with lines of nuance and
colour. Draw vibrancy
from blank canvas, a needle
taking blood. She blushes

from her skill. This map of
a land she is allowed to con-
quer, display in a drawing room.
Here it is, still held in the hoop's
halo, within the stiff circum-
ference of a world made flat.

Victorian Lampshade

Unusual to see in the tropics,
suitable for gloomy country
houses, where owners never
went to hot islands. Here,

it drips light like the moon's
udder or a melon drops
seed, one of the molluscs
on a beach with silky legs.

The urge to put a shawl on
solid objects turns a lamp
into an African Lily, a lady's
bustle. Diminishes radiance

on the drawing room talk,
while sun wilts day out
in the garden, and the rain's
tassels droop long beads.

Tea Bags

These two sachets, saddle bags which could have
been strapped on a mare the colour of Earl Grey tea.

Kick up dirt from the spoon scoop shape of horseshoes
as spindly legs trot over the Twining's Estate, India.

Who are the English to persuade steaming nations
to drink tea while they try to pour the milk of human

kindness into borders? I extract cream from a pint-
sized plastic container; it funnels into an elephant's

trunk. Outside, a tent trailer is pitched on Nettleton
Hollow; extends sides clumsy as calf's ears. Someone

safaris in bucolic Washington, CT, and I am on one
too as I drink a liquid I learned to love in a hot climate,

sip from the perpetual water lily of a Limoge cup,
saucer. Night's dark brew sifts into porous flaps of

a camper as this khaki drink sludges through, maps
my body out with memories, I raise the flag of a pinkie to.

Edgartown

Like each sea captain's home must be surrounded
by the white picket fence of a whale's jaw full of teeth
over which morning glory vines grow like scrimshaw.

Like the white cliffs of Dover must be rebuilt to welcome
ships where houses stand like blocks of marble on Main St.
and the glass fan window is a pale British Sunrise of sorts.

And the widow's walk is a wooden plank a woman paces
back and forth, back and forth, while the wind washes over
and all the roofs she sees below are overturned boats in the blue.

WATER LOGGED

Approaching Bermuda

Bermuda was founded in 1609 when the Sea Venture
was driven onto her reefs.

I think of the woman wading in, bunched skirt
held like a blown-out passenger air bag, as she
eases feet into water clear as any glass slipper.

What with the maiden voyage dashed, and reefs
drooling ocean, hungry as a dragon, Sir George Somers
needs a new move. *Sea Venture* lies on a seabed:

one of many truncated masts, hulls, a heap of
swords, shields from failed knights, approaching
Bermuda tricky. A ship's shape, the eye of a needle,

must pass through thin turquoise threads,
complex as any maze in hedged English gardens.
I think of a man rowing in, oars lift sea, wings

of a bird landing. Wigs bob in the tide like a fluther
of jellyfish. And a London legislator uses words, the bits
of straw held in the pen's beak, to build a new colony

from scratch. I think of a poet today following
this story's path, starts out for a known, but is
taken vay, vay off, *quo fata ferunt*, finds the new.

Another Reason

Another reason to live in the subtropics
is to pull hard on the linen tablecloth, step
outside, shake all breadcrumbs free, like
a rolling wave emits salt. The wrongs

said at dinner released into the air, not
left among the Spode, Limoge, Waterford.
To be swept into a straw dustpan with
the handle, a figure of a black woman,

captured in the cruelties of an island's
slave trade narrative. Another reason
to live in the sub-tropics is how mould
grows on whitewashed walls, forms

a damp map, brown, green with edges
like ones studied in geography class.
Lands before they were overtaken,
pink, flushed as if gently touched by

a sun, the same colour as roses bloom in
the mother country. A soft mildew bruise,
birthmark above the silver, hard to remove
with sunlight soap or if scoured with Clorox.

Water Logged

Not a log like Nathaniel W. Hutchings,
a sea captain, kept of weather, sea tides,
although the Longtails dip, crease the sky

which he records, resemble the dimples,
lines across her skin the coral water makes.
Neither is it the log of letters her grandfather

wrote, sent to family from London, Azores,
Jamaica. Mail spouted through the front
door letter slot like waves flow down,

or birds land before flying off again.
But rather, logged like when something
shrinks, wrinkles at edges, becomes smaller,

deflates. The sea's hand presses fingers in
to feel for ripeness to take, pluck, own, engulf,
put in a pocket, take home, leaves wobbly

prints. As if, if she stayed in, she would become
the size of a fetus again, turn in a mother's belly
over, over inside a rhythmic washing machine.

No, not logged like men in the Northwest
negotiate trees downriver, but yes, adrift,
floating away as if felled from the blue stream sky.

Wail Watch

When my cousin asks me if I want
to go look at the whales appearing
off of Coral Beach, I say no, I would

rather look for the schools of Sergeant
Majors moving like yellow and black
NYC taxis closer to shore. Rather watch

the mobile of Angelfish as they
turn in the tide. See the molluscs
on the beach with their tiny holes,

the burst buttons of the ocean which
can't contain its power. I do not
need to watch large dark mammals

with white paper party hats, tiaras for
strutting beauties, huge trucks on
a highway, to put me in touch with nature.

Although their singing has wooed me,
like lost cows trying to come home,
a resonance of my own deep wailing.

Poem to Coral Beach Club

From the terrace of Room #4 at CBC,
> *I see a faraway ruffle in the ocean,*
a thin line of white where it opens,
> *an envelope flap on the letter*
the sea keeps writing me sheet by sheet.

> *The waves turn in close to where*
I swim, swirl, a conch with messages
> *my gene code twirls, will never forget.*
The tide unravels, spreads,
> *my birth certificate, rolled out*

on flesh toned sand. Clouds above
> *in a blue so vast, endless, they do*
not move in any direction to try
> *to touch a rim in space, a place*
the universe will never curve into.

Manure, Sweat and Fennel

I ride Great Aunt Lou's thoroughbred
down Tribe Road in the August heat.

Lacquer trots, canters, drops manure.
His faeces sizzle like batter on the tar's

black skillet. Sweat marks withers and
haunches with white roped circles,

a lasso thrown to harness energy as he
clip! clops! slowly into a walk past

DeSilva's Grocery Store on Cobb's Hill.
The smell of fennel from the fields fills

my nostrils as if trailing off the French
liquor Absinthe, favoured by Parisian poets;

referred to as 'green hours' like the semi-
tropical ones Lacquer and I drink from now.

A History in Furniture

An entire empire hangs in the chintz curtain,
Ming Jars and roses suspended in a yellow
hue look as if they will never fall.

Three tropical bird prints above my bed,
like small decorative hand pistols in a drawer.
The lamp is a vase with flowers on the outside,

shade, a dowdy garden tea party hat,
light streams below in strands of fair hair.
The Chippendale chest with brass

handles: mouths, tell silence is golden,
where dark bodies of trees fell in forests
to build chairs wing-tipped as thrones,

the seated about to ascend. The ceiling
fan blade, a cricketer's bat, sends the sun's
ball away, away in every possible direction.

Erasure

Spunky with freckles, a tomboy's gaze,
she could stare down the sun,
not admit sparks penetrated epidermis,
left tiny brown tracks across a face.

A pale complexion maps out
a disappearance, a jar for cream
to erase marks surfaces, tells
how she faded away. Vanity

cosmetic to remove what is visible.
Petite as a chaser after a world en-
circling flight to follow the equator's
ring. Perhaps used to boil seawater.

She caught on fire, an Icarus fell to
an island spot on sea's wrinkled
skin, where surf bubbles beach's
seaweed edge, erodes like a blister.

The World is Not Flat

The world is not flat,
even though the horizon
mostly holds it straight.

The sea's roll tells you,
it bounces and curls.
The world is not flat

even though waves tie
white knots, hold
it down. The moon

peels curved light, reflects
arcs. The world is not
flat although the computer

screen makes it one
dimensional, prints it
out into a sheet of paper.

STAR MAP

Summer's Widow

Dressed to kill, the maple is full of gold,
red, yellow. If you are going to die
be beautiful in the moment. Let wind
lift you in a last dance that reveals
the curvaceous reach of your branches.

If you age, age well, and cause envy
from the audience. Before you drop,
surprise everyone with your complexity.
Don't go quietly out but howl with
a presence before letting go.

And if that isn't enough, just reappear!
A ghost rising up the long thin trunk
of a chimney's neck with smoke
unfurling and spreading leaves,
reaching across the entire sky.

Moccasin

Indian summer
turns the yard
into patches
of brown and grey,
an Appaloosa's flank.

Bright yellow leaf,
a feather
from a squaw
passing.

The woods
all hush and quiet,
a season moves
in moccasins.

Trees light presences
here then gone,
leave the sun's ring exposed,
a campfire still smoking.

Change

The first leaves have turned
here in the hollow
at the bottom of a low branch.

These bright patches
are coins in a deep pocket
waiting to be spent.

The first tithes
for the season ahead
of constant change.

An early bet placed
with a handful of money
to win a toppling sum
of gold piled to the sky.

In Hock

Leaves cover the ground.
I have enough pawn tickets
to get the sun out of hock
every winter night,
every winter night cold surrounds it.

It reappears each a.m. in
the thinned hand of the bare tree,
a magician's trick
to make a coin
come out of the blue.

I can't believe it is there,
until warm fingers
touch my back, arms and legs,
planted down in spring's soft earth
with the spindly roots of shadow.

Falling

A hard time to fall in love,
what with the landscape
letting go, letting go, releasing,
nothing is permanent. Leaves

are everywhere, hands cut
off from holding onto, trying to
steal too much sky. The sun
litters too, throwing parts

of itself away, pieces of it
still shine everywhere. Is
this love's work? To be made
naked, vulnerable, stripped

to the core. I stand like a tree
amongst debris. A passenger
who has discarded all tickets
to any other destination.

Cruel Enough

That the trees have become wallflowers
against the dim sky, stand in a shirking
beauty, all limbs and chipped bark.

Cruel enough, but snow makes all
white! A blank, no references.
Cruel enough, stiff colonial houses,

clouds of incense rise from chimneys,
purge environs, smoke twines into a rope,
an escape to heaven. Cruel enough a publisher

says most poetry books end up as pulp like
the shredded ice now landing everywhere,
but so cruel I have to write this poem about it.

Simply the Fourth

A flag a child could draw, so right for such a young country.
No emblems, or crowns, just a bunch of stars to reach for,
and the fast lines of movement for roads anyone can find.

The food is simply cooked around a fire from early days.
Meat made grabbable in buns, soft in the hand like a
   catcher's mitt.
Chips break in the mouth, hosts for the moment's celebration.

Likewise, firecrackers shoot above and then fade quickly,
party souvenirs thrown away in the bin. Everyone wears T-
shirts, sandals, baseball caps. Nothing impedes going forth.

Ripe

My Saab smells like a ripe cheese
inside, a triple crème at full age.
Yellow tennis balls are from some sort
of fondue. Orange plastic trainer,

a goat milk variety, sprouts
knobby spores. My dog stinks,
like seaweed on the beach, coat
wet days after a swim. It is too soon

for summer to rot, sour. August
claustrophobic, tree trunks,
L.P. record holders spin the season's
green vinyl disk, over, over again.

Snowfall

I think of what we cannot hold,
claim, although it might lie
down flat and white
as linens folded in a drawer.

Even those boxes of wood
stacked in a bureau become coffins,
where the fabric inside frays
like the tattered skin of a person's body.

Even when we put a mothball in,
small as a moon to prevent darkness,
and vacant as an evil eye
for anyone who would try to rob a grave.

Cornfield Early Spring

All vertebrae and broken bones
pulled out of their sockets
from the weight of death.

Corn stalks matted as
the hair of a corpse,
dry leaves curl like maggots.

Cobs discarded from the cold's
machinery like old radio batteries.
This is where winter got wrecked.

Wrought Iron Bed

The 'Estate Sale' sign misleads,
there are only a few pieces of furniture
in the driveway of an old farm.

Wrought iron headboard, footboard
painted white like a stream of milk
flows through machinery while

the hired hands sleep. The steely
outline of angel wings come to
lift the tired away from daily toil.

Two gates: one keeps a dreamer
penned in, one swings open, leads
cows up to a high green meadow.

ISLAND-BOUND MAIL

Lockets

Cousin Wendy tells me when we
grew up on Bermuda, we were like
mid-twentieth-century mutes in a *Sea
Venture*, caught between a rock or two.

I say *Yes! We let the ocean fill our ears, like
conches before we spoke.* Mutes in a mutiny
against linear language, the death walk
piracy plank of the horizon's flattened edge.

Sound curled our veins, the vines of Allamanda
trumpets clinging to limestone homes,
hung on with jump rope feet. Learned syntax
ebbed, flowed, brought in, out with petticoat

turns, the swish of a silk skirt, and yes!
Left shells the tide broke through like lockets.
Mutes until words mutated, found
the norm to catch the cusp of circles,

Hurricane Emily's eye, her spheres,
and the returning silence from what is
spun out to edges, the clothes petal
softened from a constant cycle of wash.

House Visit

Cousin Tina tells me I can have my pick
of china pieces on a mahogany table.
They rise like rose corals, stuck to
a reef. The house now has a deep

sea feel, shafts of light bounce
off of mirrors, surf crashes and
slipcovers, bureaus are stripped
of buttons, handles as if an interior

life no longer exists, everything open,
up for grabs. As if currents rushed
through, left books, drawers on floors.
My great Aunt Susie took tea in the side

garden. Harriet carrying the tray of
silver, a game of chess where each
part is thoughtfully placed. I remember
the rough image of *Pearl,* the lost

family ship, etched into the side
of the house, a child's finger drawing
or one drawn in sand by a stick, the ocean
removes layer by layer as it polishes

the sand into the sheen of a tidy
housekeeper. Each ruffle of tide
luminous as a shell, where grit spins
into a jewel deep inside an oyster.

I is for Immigrant

The vertical you become
leaving your country.

I is for how you see
differently, eye pupils learn

another country. I is for
I'm a migrant now. I is

for the two stitches sewn
across a border, top one

holds the fray of exit,
bottom, the pull of return.

Falling in Love with My Father in the Snow

Because when we came to America
the landscape was black and white,
snow and dark bark like the blotted print of
the New York Times he read on Sundays.

Because he brought us here in January,
when sleet swept across the horizon
like a curtain to erase what I had
known before, the colours of an island.

Because when he held the steering wheel
in his hand, like a faucet he could turn off,
on, he was so happy as the traffic rushed
by in streams of water he was so thirsty for.

Island-Bound Mail

The sign at the Post Office
shows what a terrorist
package might look like.

Just like the one I send,
has a clump of stamps in
the shape of Matisse's Snail.

A school of fish swims
the front, headed up
for the surface. Bits of

Scotch tape here, there,
like a snapper scaled.
And the loose brown

package paper, a sweater
a sibling hands down
to you, big, baggy,

the Shetland Wool
unravels into the string
wound round and round.

The postmistress asks if
anything is explosive
inside. I want to say, *Yes!*

*Books have been known
to cause revolutions, pages
turning fan many a fire!*

The non-terrorist package
has the US Postal Eagle.
Swift, eyes anything out

of uniform, what strays across
lines, roams 3rd class mail, it
is eager to pick up in tallows.

Shakespearean

We stare at the jaws of the white shark,
teeth sharp as cut diamonds for
a Harry Winston necklace.

They must have had their own
beauty shimmering in the silk
of the dark undersea, a tiara.

But we cannot look without
seeing ribbons of red, the un-packaged
human. Neither can we look

at its snare without remembering
the slaves harvesting bright jewels
in a dark pit in Africa. Beauty

and treachery so close, so
much a part of the ocean where
the lionfish, dazzling as

a sequined evening purse,
hordes and steals, floats
in with its Shakespearean collar.

Painted Woman

after Cecily Brown

Paint her in, seal the edges of her
bare body, drop paint on her, like
a sinker on a fishing line drowns

the hook. Make sure she can't
breathe, can barely turn to look at
you, her Master. I would rather

a woman paint another naked:
waves of high pink, choppy as
an ocean, push the frame's eddies.

The subject spread across the canvas:
the geography of acute sensations
a nude is when her skin is touched.

Rocking the Fixer

It is what is not in the photograph
we respond to. The spaces in the island
landscape not built up, still full of palms,
cedars, oleanders. The sailboats in the

distance like a row of tents on the horizon,
or a line of Tibetan flags taut with the absence
in between. The sun blotchy as a streaked
darkroom chemical. I remember rocking

the fixer tray as images surface in a cradle,
a distorted swimmer comes to the top of
water in the harbour. The Westclox Timer
with numerals large as the ones used in

a nursery to teach a child to count.
The loud *Tick! Tock!* as if time is a wind
up toy, one can turn back, forward like
black and white film on sprockets in

my Leica. Capture, push the button
down, a thumb tack made of steel.
So the shutter unfolds its creased
wings like a raven, before it flies.

Camel

Funny-looking as any apparition
a desert mind could have, dune-

coloured humps pitched like
tents on sticks. Curves slope

into the teapot's ceremonial
spout full of amber liquid.

Eyelids, lashes curl back from
the heat of flirting with the sun.

Lips large enough to drink water
from any blue and dry and dusty sky.

BOILING HOT

Antique Star Map

Round as a crystal ball,
one might turn to find a path,
hold in one's hand, cup
a drop in the ocean. This one

has a star in the middle, like
a Bermuda Sand Dollar I
would find on Coral Beach,
the tides washed over, spent.

A pin cushion where precise
points prick the dark. A child's
circle of marbles, large planets
knock out smaller ones: taws

hit peewees. The nineteenth century
one is full of flying figures, a Sistine
Chapel for ship captains, where one
looks up to feel the muscle of

myths ripple the heavens.
Capricorn's bow and arrow,
a shipmate's sextant used to negotiate
the skies, to find a seaworthy mark.

Seahorse

No need for wings or legs
in the buoyant tide of the ocean.

Like the *f* hole in a cello
where the music seeps through.

Miscellaneous notes in the waves'
symphony. Shaped like a pick I

used to clean Lacquer's hooves,
removed earth from the iron

shoe so he could soar higher
when sweat poured down,

his back salty as the ocean's
surf, smelling of the undersea.

Snake Skin

We all leave traces of ourselves,
the old blouse in the dryer circles,

a hamster in a cage. Strips of skin
on the stone walk, flat as condoms.

One dribbles from the wall, saliva
from a mouth, Moses' parched water

emits from stone. Like a train rushes
through a tunnel, the serpent comes

out on time. The repeated shedding
leaves a tape measure of what it was.

Thin wings of renewal, the inverse,
of shadow, an umbilical cord ripples light.

Silver-tongued as ever, like the sword
guarding Eden flashes back and forth.

Buoy

If you are going to leave your island,
better do it on a ship, where you see
the water between the dock and your
liner extend into the crease of waves,

open like an accordion. Feel your
heart roll back, forth, a buoy tethered to
the wharf. If you must leave your country,
better a seaborne way, the tilt of

swells rock you inconsolable, like
in a nanny's crib. Better than by
plane where through a tiny window
like your diving mask of youth, the hook

isle drops away, the sinker you watch
disappear into harbour waters when
you fished off Paget Ferry. Better
a boat that stole many an ancestor into

the blue, so when you pour the sludge
of Earl Grey from a silver teapot like
muddy water from an elephant trunk,
it holds all memories that slosh inside, still.

Words that Curve and Curl

Words that curve and curl
from the sea, the tide, dampness,
get into everything. The seaweed
clings to your calf when you
walk out of the water, like varicose
veins as you return to land legs.

Words that curve and curl, like the conch,
Allamanda petals, the roundabout
where Mobylettes, Zundaps, Morris
Minors swish by, fish in a current.
Words that curve and curl, collect
the island dead centre as in the eye

of a hurricane. Don't sit up straight
on the page like for a class at B.H.S.
Overflow into the world like when I
jumped overboard in Paget Harbour
caused rivulets which rocked boats,
like anchors wanting to tipsy into the ocean.

Rudder

Like a Good Friday kite
which flew too far out of
sky-bound realms, the mast
and sail tattered on the seabed is

finally at rest. Rows of
barnacles like nails screwed
in to keep it still, steady.
We all want to find permanence.

A ship captain relative was
buried at sea in an un-floatable
coffin. The white breaking surf
parted open as it entered the deep.

The only wings seen to rescue
him, although sea fans flourished
on the top, like one his widow waved
back, forth, a rudder to direct her grief.

Recorded

She preferred the days the light
shimmered off the snow like
on a South Shore beach, Bermuda.

Watched the Tompkins men
shovel the path, the blur of
ice over their shoulder a wave

one bobbed in as a child for hours,
or like a towel thrown on one's back
while walking out from the water.

The white, white sleet billows
around the 1814 saltbox house,
a mast pulling it into the deep.

The non-negotiable horizon, driven
away like the bright sun made it so
as her sea captain ancestor recorded.

Ship Clock

for Nancy Christina Hutchings

I hold it up to cousin Tina, the Westclox
wall clock in a St. George's supply
store, and say it is like a porthole
with the sea lapping its blue rim,

will keep BDA time when I am in
America. The second hand like
the shadow on a sundial at Hillcrest
circling, cuts light, sharp as a shark's fin,

a Pinocchio nose as the day
elongates its boundary of truth.
Where is it? Not here, nor
there. I remember the ship clock

at Greystones, turns in the glass
case, an earring, time's immediate
jewel. Multiple bells ring, the ocean's
ripples when an anchor strikes deep.

Punt

I have to notice the white
three-levelled bookshelf I
order is like a wooden punt,

blunt, simple, occupies space
without notice. Remember
sitting in the middle of mine,

rowing Ely's Harbour. Each
oar pulling up water like
an open book with clear pages.

Handles forming an arrowhead
either way. Out to sea, back
to the beach. I was thick in

the plot of the afternoon,
my back like any binding
to a text having to endure

the opening, the closing of
the strokes against the tide,
the weight of the full meaning.

Boiling Hot

She rubs the silver pot with
Gorham's polish as if her genie
was inside, would waft out from
the steam island tea makes

in such a humid climate. Prepares
triangle sandwiches, lops off
dark crusts that heap on the kitchen
counter as if caterpillars crawled out

from frilly lettuce leaves, like sea's
wavy rim, the silk cap sleeves on
smocked dresses made for the misses.
Arranges a square like the cross

intersection of the Amen Corner in Paget,
a treacherous passage through.
Dons white gloves used for church
and to serve among the fair English.

Watches their skin turn earth-brown,
the harsh light claiming a geography
of persons the Empire sent across
the world. The British sunrise on

every commoner's door back in
London, an unblinking watchful eye,
a fan spread wide open to
cool down boiling hot countries.

Side Saddle

She sits like a mermaid in
a side saddle, a kind of
extra dish to compliment
the main. Dangerous not

to use both legs, be off
balance, tilt the horse
one way with too heavy
a burden, a sack thrown

over a hook. Pegasus with
one wing, like a seal lunges
towards the frothy surf of
the mane. The spread thighs

saved for one occupation,
or the other where birth
stirrups come to mind. Let
her post in sync with ups,

downs, slip the soft slide
canter, shoehorn her
forward, the full throttle
gallop, her power out of

the gates, she leans into
the reins' horizon line, pulls
the snaffle bit in the horse's
mouth: wishboning her will.

TIDE TABLES

Every Civilization

Needs its pillars,
the rubber tree
is such in Coral Beach Club's domain.

Below, the roots pile like
dead bones from an excavation,
brown leaves archival paper

to pick up artifacts. I was
civilized here. The silver urn
for tea placed ritualistically on

the linen tablecloth as if
an altar. Liquid the colour
of elastic downpours into

an elephant's trunk in
an empire where all
human memory was stretched.

A Geography of Tea

The kettle's high pitch,
a vexing against *all* ills,
the village women's *hiss,*
wards off evil. The shrill

sound of the wind whipping
casuarinas as a hurricane
circles the island. This
bitter brew we savour,

put in sugar, cream, make
sweet. Indian tea pickers carry
a basket on their back, thrust
leaves over their shoulders in

a reversal of the child's tipsy
game. *I'm a little teapot,*
short and stout, tip me over
and pour me out. The thick

green bushes grow like pieces
of a puzzled map where
countries try to join. Upstairs
china is fine enough for hot

chai to go in first, won't crack.
Downstairs crockery breaks
without milk first in a cup, like
a doily from the mother country.

England Taught Me

England taught me to love the rain,
the privacy it provides,
long tassled drops on the Victorian
umbrella's edge of empire.

The splash of footsteps, waves made,
not allowed. There the quiet whispery
life, where even the sun must need
these rosary strands of water for penance.

For being too bright, noticeable above,
creating the shadow grave of a person,
doing the ordinary. To remind them, hurry
up. Here is death's dark angel hovering.

Opening Up the Legal Year 2018

The wigs take the law into the feminine,
men and women long-haired.

As if a bit of surf got attached
to their forehead, skull, rhythms of

South Shore guide them as
they sit in cedar partitions like

levees the ocean might crash
through. Okay, we all know the sea

is the subconscious, so here it is
symbolized in the new legal year,

keeping up habits of the old. I
think they all look like their locks

are still in rollers, haven't gotten
quite awake enough yet to work.

Still sea rocked by the maritime deep,
lulled by the hushes of a mother soothing.

To Keep the Light

She raises her skirt
like a folded sail
as she ascends the
conch spiralled staircase,
full of the sky's
dizzy whisperings.

The flame of the large
lamp, a needle's eye in
the rags of the clouds
she watches. A sea captain
to see what a storm brings,
full of lightning's stitching.

The spinning steps up,
causes a dervish
trance, the ecstasy of
circling. The latitude,
longitude cut of flashes,
the golden pigtail of a girl twirls.

Because You Were Taught to Look

Because you were taught to look
and not to see, you raised the camera
to your eye, a protective mask
to grind the world down in one lens.

Because you were taught to look
and not to see, the paint brush
slowly lifted its torch of paint
into the cave of a canvas wall.

Because you were taught to look
and not to see, words shadow
the page, can only define
the space of light around them.

Mosquito Net at Elma Napier's Estate

The mosquito net above the bed,
ghost of a writer who once visited her.

The spirit leaves the body above a caved
in mattress, sunken, about to collapse.

So many fictions dreamt on it. The muslin
ties at the bottom, like a mango heavy in

a string market bag she bought in Baptiste.
Hangs like an exclamation mark for

the filmy subconscious more vivid than
the mountain view outside the window

and more present than the mosquitos
gathering on its airy white slopes at night.

Not the Country I Was Born In

So no straightforward monotone,
just raised up high pitches, like a pinkie
for tea, and then melting words,
breadfruit which couldn't survive heat,

sticky. A snapper flipping on a dock in
a pool of water, like a tongue
still full of the sea's rhythms
seeking an ocean's context.

A sentence as something to end?
Not so in the semi-tropics, enough
just to begin. In the U.K., a course
to jump your horse through for the

Queen. Not this U.S. banner for the self,
Chinese Cookie blurb about truest
you with lips pursed for a kiss.
This is not the country I was born in.

Tide Tables

Each day I read the tide tables
in the Mid Ocean News. The graph
pitched like a sail in the right angle
of the square columns. Overnight

a spider had spun a raggedy web
in a corner. I was always aware
of the high tide/low tide shift, as if
the island balanced itself on the tip

of a volcano. Low tide harbour,
high tide South Shore, high tide
harbour, low tide South Shore.
I read your in/out breathing

as it daily rose, fell, an inward
current, still here, still eager
for oxygen to infuse a body
with life. Your mouth gaped

open in an o, like a coin that
would drop into the splash
of your chest as it drew air in,
out. The oxygen machine puttering,

the sound of the ferry boat *Georgia*
idling at the Paget Dock, about to
resume its ride into Hamilton.
The last night of your breathing,

when I watched the crest of your
chest, rise, fall, when it told me
everything of how long you
would be lingering here, your

left lower rib so thin, as it went
up and down, the curve of your
bones pulling up flesh was a small
bird about to leave its nest, fly.

LATITUDE, LONGITUDE

Ode to Sappho

Thank you for leaving fragments,
'the shards of language' as Walcott says,
like what falls away from a poem
and is not understood, a few lines,
fragment of memory, ghostly as a ship-
wreck broken apart in tropical seas.

Thank you for leaving fragments,
a phrase, the poem's true meaning,
not just the part it plays: the anole
lizard's dewlap flashing into
an orange bud, the cereus
blooming within its one night.

Thank you for leaving fragments,
I am exiled from my past, poems
piecemeal, ocean-drenched ruins,
random mollusc shells I collect,
sea-surfaced, shattered, momentarily
brighten the tide's curving line.

Walcott's Lament

Said off-island, he became
disoriented. I, too, miss
the sea's rocking back, forth.
I'm a metronome, keep its time.

The spasmic white surf
girdling the land holds
it in tight, shrinks me into
a landscape, I fit. Queen Palms

turn the sky into a vaulted
Gothic ceiling, like it too wants
mooring, to remain in place,
above the ocean's shifting blue.

Sun Spots

The shredded light my straw
hat shed was like grains of
wheat falling on my shoulders

from the crown's stout silo.
I was a fruit ripening in
semitropical heat. Now spots,

like seeds inside, implode,
grow their own geography,
a chain of Caribbean islands

surface, link over my chest,
tattoo for the sun's expeditions.
One, the size of a shilling, blood

money spent for a golden tan
the regal feel of its glow, the silky
sensation, summer is my skin.

House of Mirrors

The slap, slap of the wave
against sand, sound of
a woman kneading pastry,
the tide rimmed as a crust.

The underwater house of
mirrors, torsos swell into
Willendorf Venuses and
a jellyfish floats adrift like

an auntie's church hanky.
The urge to float constant,
remain aloft before the wave
throws an arm over

my shoulder to enlist me,
spins my body around
a turbulent wringer in deep
wash currents. Tiny molluscs

litter my footprints as I
come out of the tide like
false toenails I shed as I
regain my landlocked stride.

I have sand in my hair,
papier-mâché strands,
stiffening locks like a jester's
hat I have had to adorn.

Island Wave

The taxi driver beeps the horn,
raises his forefinger above
the steering wheel: the Bermuda wave.

Like the island's Skink lizard,
peering above a banana leaf,
just enough effort. On old British

racing green Morris Minors,
the traffic signals would open
on each side, like the dewlap

the anole displays for mating and
to be territorial. The National
Geographic article says they change

skin for camouflage when in
new terrain, like the sun patterns of
shadow and light on the car's roof conceals

passengers in its daily hide and seek
game, although each a.m. its fiery long
digits hail, hail at us from the earth's edge.

Jigsaw

Like pieces of a jigsaw puzzle,
reefs around the island, a part

of the whole on the tablecloth
of the Atlantic. I sit on the beach,

each wave crested forms into
the White Cliffs of Dover, origins

of the island culture when ship-
wrecked ancestors landed from

a boat bashed apart like a native paw
paw, scattered seeds from which I grew.

Sea salted with an inner rhythm
perpetually rocked by the undertow,

the low pitch sound of a pull back
tide down into the celestial deep.

Pink Wall Clock

Like island time it slows
down, as if a pie where
the knife gets stuck
in the Suriname cherry filling,

the hand becomes weighted,
wobbly. The numbers, years
marked in icing on a child's
birthday cake. Hours passing,

flamingo stick-figure legs
stride. The Empire sun sets,
all magenta skies and lacy clouds,
a strawberries and cream dessert.

Sun Prayers

The images of the deceased African
Bermudians in the Royal Gazette
were heartwarming to me. Photo

complete with bio underneath,
like cricket trading cards in death's
ultimate out of the Somerset Stadium

game. Badges to get on the *People
get ready, there's a train
a-coming!* for the above-the-ground

railroad trail. I want their faith
when I die. I want the dialect tones
of their voices, soft sun prayers

of sea wave sounds and lightning
strikes, weather cutting the landscape
in two. Brimming with a habitation's

sea-weedy shores and habits. Lazy
moments when a tongue curls in heat,
a flame in a sermon's slow fire. About

the home of oleander maiden hills,
the marshy toad land, the fossilized
limestone earth where a body will

finally lie. Curved rib bones, like
scaffolding of the ships that brought
us here. I want these saints present.

Winter Survival

Let the bright white light
cascading through your home
in search of colour, show you
you always wanted to paint
your sorry trashcans, battered
silver-grey from a long war

of use, the colour of a mango.
When you spray the liquid, you
become a hibiscus blooming a petal.
When you hold up the orange tin-
can top, it is a shield against the cold.
And then when you must also colour

the condiment shelves yellow, it
is like the island sun reviving
your own senses. The island must
always be near. More so in the snow,
heaped like a rolled-up canvas against
your home's edge which invites filling.

Leonora's Landscape

A relief to know the Mexicans talk to the dead,
so many ghosts in Europe after the wars. Here, I feel
I am in one of my landscapes, Muertos face paintings,
green cacti, burro taxis, seen in one glance. I was told Surrealism
was born because of the camera. The lens' winking eye
fooled the world. I think after two World Wars, one
goes crazy, stretches figures across a canvas like a torture rack.

In the market today peasants beat a pinata, like my prayers
pelted God in Spain when I was insane, demanded treats after
Max's arrest. Here, roadside altars to Mary abound, replicate
kiosks in my English village, Madonna called on for the day's
errands. Cuernavaca pilgrims balance skulls on sticks, like balls
in a circus, play with the deceased. I remember tombstones in
the family cemetery at Clayton, shields we propped up
  against death.

The Poem is Here

Where the geranium leaves yellow
into a coward's colour, as I have made
them one from over-watering, dependent.

In the thin frail trail of clouds above
the lake's beach, as if the backbone of
the sky is withered by such balmy heat.

The poem is here, where the side mirrors
on my Jag flash light like duelling swords
for the road's trail ahead, and the sun

rolls around in the opening in the roof,
like a ball in a box, bouncing from
the thrust of speed, unable to remain in borders.

PINK TYPEWRITER

Maidenhead

In the video taken from
above, the round reefs
off Coral Beach emit surf
like dark pots boiling on
a stove, a sea pudding

squirting. The fume and fury
of tide I have gotten caught in,
jumped up and down
in its bob, like playing
skip rope to duck the fringed

line of the surf's coil as
its flows over. The pull between
beach and the outer sea intense.
Swimming over the top
of a wave as it swells up,

a confrontation, like climbing
a glassy mountain. Sometimes,
I let it carry me in on its prow,
a maidenhead on an ancestor's
ship, as it takes me into shore.

Home, Home

Is what the poets from the Caribbean,
Anguilla, Barbados and Jamaica, call
their island, which is what Bermuda is
for me, although I live stateside.

Because I learned the female's frilly
strength in the tide of waves which
repeatedly scroll into the sea's backbone,
white and gnarled, skeletal as unwrapped bones

on an archaeological dig, but also alive, bending
with the undertow's shift. Where I learned
life's pace from the speed of jellyfish
flapping like a bird in the sea's sky

with no landing, no touchdown place.
All itself in the haloed petticoats of moments,
like masts billowing full of a home, home,
the journey of myself to an isle in a turquoise ocean.

Home

The way a Bermudian says
home, holding onto the 'o',
humming its tune. Closing
lips down on the 'me'. Home,

personal, inside. The way
the tone goes down after 'ho'
from *Hi! Ho!* ship sailing days
with a bit of *Land Ahoy!* A hoe

arrivants used to break open
the island's fresh soil. The way
a Bermudian says home, like
a harmonica with a sweet long song.

Allamanda

Well, a British sun bonnet and
also a sun, exaggerated, drooping
in its own heat. The mouth of
yellow, sweet as butter melting.

The swell of the skirt of a lady
in Louis XIV court, the Solar King
of France, making them tilt, need
an extravagant hairdo to balance.

Reminds me of blowfish puffing,
the way one loses one's breath in
the warmth, bell-like in shape,
humidity's silent chiming.

Underwater Flight

The fan corals look
like wings, flutter atop
the reef as I float, fly by,

aware of stasis, aware
of flight in a subterranean
aqua sky. The finger coral,

delectable as cheese
curls, the angelfish,
bream, snappers nibble.

The brain coral,
a mind picturing
the zig zag graphics of

a Keith Haring painting.
A light bulb goes
off in the deep. How

could such a space
form me? Turned Cyclops
by my mask, a madness

necessary to see with
right, left eyes conjoined.
This layered place of

sprawling order, a sifting
sand domain, eelgrasses
drift in long strips. Ribbons

trail the depths of
what shifts, remains in
the ocean's constant opening.

Tribe Roads

The eastern light so bright, Maurice, the taxi
driver, motoring the South Shore into Paget,
pulls down the overhead windshield flap,
places a pirate patch on the sun's eye.

In the summer months, the surrey with
the fringe on top; tassels drip like surf
breaking on the shore, cools down the local
passengers. The oval microphone in his

hand, Maurice tells the woman radio
operator managing call-ins where he is,
as the cord spirals with places he
annunciates, knows. The somersaulting

way routes of an island coil like waves
on the beach, repetitive, circling one's
days, times, memory, an umbilical cord
tugging home, no matter the destination.

Pink Typewriter

"You sveet me," locals say to one another;
like dialect sveetens me, nation, natal
language returns me to honey sound days.

My typewriter, the colour pink of Dunkley
Dairy's strawberry ice cream, very cotton
candy, with alphabet keys held inside

a metal frame, like a mouth full
of sugar cubes, helps to write
the sun-tongue swoon of childhood days.

My fingers, chubby as overweight legs
on a gym stairs machine, have to strike
down hard; each rung rises like a scythe

ready to cut cane. Letters on a poem's
page, ants on a wall in a humid
Bermuda kitchen, trailing towards

Crow Lane Bakery Banana Bread
left on the counter to cool. Sheets
of paper pour from the Royal

Classic carriage, roll out like slabs
of sticky icing for White Coconut Cake,
porous as the island's limestone.

Fair

The bruise from Mohs surgery
on my left cheekbone is red,
a stop light to any more sun;

then green as the veins open up
blood, rush to negotiate the intricate
traffic between a heart and a public face.

How lovely all that semitropical
light felt. Now the site turns yellow as
a last memory of a golden hue fades.

What made us, post-Victorian era, seek
to be robed in such earthiness, toss
our parasols aside? Their tipped point

a nipple on the breast of the mother
country, preserving milk-white skin
beneath, the fair visage of her daughters.

A Small White World

Like the famed Bermuda Triangle, the one
the presenter notes on the Savage Map of
the Tucker's Town cemetery, where many dead

were buried, is also one within which many African
Bermudians disappeared, and the thin oblong
outline later designated for the official burial site

is tombstone shaped, as if to mark the permanence
of a removal, the death of lived history on
the Mid Ocean Club land. And the golf balls

pinging against the remaining gravestones are symbolic
of a small white world at leisure hitting a Dunlop
onto the bones of the dead. And in the archived photo,

all the original stone markers with shield ferns
are like reefs surrounding the isle with anemone
seaweed protecting us, our isle, from oblivion.

Gombey Fire

The fire rises like the headdress
of the Gombey dancing
Front Street. The wooden
logs play their crackling
beat, heat up the entire house,

like the vibrancy of dancers
bring a mirthful frenzy to Hamilton.
The flame jumps the way
the leader springs in procession.
The fiery colours as bright as

mirrors reflecting island sun
on cloaks. The sparks brighten
the hearth like when Gombey
perform slave narratives, bring
light into our darkened history.

Flag

The Nigerian woman wailing in
the inflated rescue boat is beating
the floor, kicking, hitting it with arms,
legs, like a child throwing a tantrum

who wants her doll. She has lost
her baby in the Mediterranean Sea,
the sides of the craft, the swollen lips
of the ocean's mouth howling for her.

The tide rocks slowly to comfort her, ease
the pain. From above, the heads of refugees
crammed into vessels look like seeds
in a pod waiting to be planted on new

land. The thin bodies of the dead found
on Lesvos beaches, Sokoto tribal clothes
wrapped around skeletal frames, each
corpse, like a flag for the country sought.

Coronavirus Moon

Like the coronavirus, circular,
bright, the pink moon floats
pandemic skies to soothe. Covid-19,

spikey as a coral off of South Shore,
located on reefs we swam
over with our masks, snorkels

to help us breathe, wafts the air;
like the lionfish coming in for
a kill, invader of seas. Bermudians look

at the lunar globe over Hamilton,
the sound of a camera shutter slowly
clicking, a tranquilizer is swallowed.

Sea Wise

Putting on my Covid-19 mask
reminds me of the one
I used floating semitropical
seas as a child in Bermuda.

The Cephalopods off the dock
a favourite to watch. One
moment an octopus floats
the clear blue, streams long

tentacles, like a mophead
cleaning. Another moment
is a star above the reef, arms
raised up, suckers, lightbulbs

on a chandelier. Disappears
into the rocks, a silky handkerchief
tucked in for an emergency. I
recall the shape shifting to stay

alive which sea-wise Bermudians
adapt as we cover island smiles,
have laughter muffled, stand apart,
lest we become one another's predator.

Landfall

The diagram in the Royal Gazette
of Hurricane Paulette billows like
a parachute landfalling on Bermuda.
The National Geographic photo is of

the tortoise caught in a plastic bag
as if sneezing a ghostly phlegm.
Climate change is a bad poem, full of
mixed metaphors which do not resonate.

An artist makes collages of debris
she finds on beaches, ghost sticks
from fishing nets, thin as bones of
the dead, soon to be extinct species.

She says that sandals, sneakers,
flip flops are everywhere, a trail
of our footprints that the waves
can't erase to make the shores pristine.

London Taxi Windshield Wipers

So sensitive, they lift before
a downpour, like a husband might
finish a wife's sentence, so in tune.

Rise up with the stream of rain
cascading like hair, a princess awakened
by the kiss of her inner prince. The wipers

blink above my Mini dashboard, as
I rouse myself into the sleeping memory
of London streets, where downpours

train pedestrians into a courteous
privacy, so used to living inside
the chapeled spaces of weather.

Riding in from Heathrow, cabs
purring from diesel, wipers scrape
the windshield the way a painter removes

paint from an overworked canvas,
so a new vision can be present,
a fresh way of seeing into the world.

Fontana Degli Artisti

Like novena prayer cards to aid the way,
a friend sends me her photos of Roma.
Stone statues melt into liquid fountains
under the warm Italian sun and air.

A necklace of pearls streams from
the mouth of the Fontana Degli
Artisti. An ancient sense of what
is held, gushes up from time's wells.

Bachelard said: "All language must
contain water." And as ink spills
from my pen, I water-witch, conduct
the next source for my poems, find what

is under the paper-white page, blocky
as a piece of marble. And like Moses
hitting a rock with Aaron's rod, my typewriter
key strikes it hard for words to flow, flourish.

Acknowledgements

Conch (Bermuda Arts Council Grant, 2002)

Salt: 'Conch', 'Tea Service', 'Devonshire Moon', 'Banana Bunch'
The Royal Gazette: 'Pearl'

Somersault (Guernica Editions, 2015)

The Caribbean Writer: 'A History of Knives', 'Jelly Fish'
Dalhousie Review: 'Elephant Horn', 'Nova Scotia Skills'
Edinburgh Review: 'Ear Drum'
The Fiddlehead: 'Ebury Court Hotel'
International Literary Quarterly: 'Navel String'
Journal of Caribbean Literatures: 'Somersault'
Womanspeak: Journal of Art and Literature by Caribbean
    Women: 'Postcolonial Pie'

Because There Was No Sea (Anaphora Literary Press, 2014)

Agenda: 'Airport Necklace'
Bermuda Anthology of Poetry: 'Phone Cord'
Buechner Society of Bermuda: 'The Sunday Times'
International Literary Quarterly: 'Because There Was No Sea'
Magma: 'Olivetti'
The Moth: 'Practice'
Numero Cinq: 'Nothing'
Postcolonial Text: 'Blue Blood'
Theodate: 'Seasick'

Immigrant's Autumn (Aldrich Press, 2014)

Agenda: 'Falling in Love with a Lake'
The Arts Journal of Guyana: 'Jump Rope on Court Street',
    'Lionfish', 'Cruel Work'
Journal of Postcolonial Writing: 'Salinas'
MOKO: Journal of Caribbean Arts and Letters: 'Tea Bags',
    'Lighthouse Keeping'
Open Roads Review: 'Victorian Lampshade'
New Welsh Review: 'We Didn't Know Yet'
The Toronto Quarterly: 'This Is Not Your Ticket'
The Vineyard Gazette: 'Edgartown'

Water Logged (Aldrich Press, 2016)

The Bermudian: 'Water Logged'
Buechner Society of Bermuda Journal: 'Manure, Sweat and
    Fennel'
The Caribbean Writer: 'Another Reason'
Free Verse Journal: 'A History in Furniture'
Poetry Salzburg Review: 'Erasure', 'The World is Not Flat'
Poui: 'Wail Watch', 'Poem to Coral Beach'
Tongues of the Ocean: 'Approaching Bermuda'

Star Map (FutureCycle Press, 2016)

The Country and Abroad: 'Summer's Widow', 'Moccasin',
    'Change', 'In Hock', 'Falling'
Poetry Salzburg Review: 'Simply the Fourth', 'Cruel Enough',
    'Ripe'
Seek It Anthology on Sleep: 'Wrought Iron Bed'
Stand: 'Snowfall', 'Cornfield'

Island Bound Mail (Kelsay Books, 2017)

The Country and Abroad: 'Island Bound Mail'
Interviewing The Caribbean: 'What is Shade'
The Missing Slate: 'Lockets'
A New Ulster: 'Falling in Love with My Father in the Snow'
Papercuts: 'Painted Woman'
Poems of Pacuare Anthology: 'Camels'
Poui: 'I is for Immigrant', 'House Visit', 'Shakespearean'
Words on Waves Anthology: 'Rocking the Fixer'

Boiling Hot (Kelsay Books, 2018)

Agenda: 'Seahorse', 'Snakeskin'
Ambit: 'Punt', 'Sea Clock'
Anomaly: 'Recorded'
Art Ascent: 'Words that Curve and Curl'
Postcolonial Text: 'Antique Star Map', 'Boiling Hot', 'Buoy'
Poui: 'Rudder'
Southword: 'Side Saddle'

Tide Tables (Kelsay Books, 2019)

The Caribbean Writer: 'Every Civilization', 'Tide Tables'
Dodging The Rain: 'England Taught Me', 'To Keep the Light',
  'Because You Were Taught to Look'
MOKO: 'Welcoming in the New Legal Year 2018'
Poetry Ireland Review: 'Mosquito Net at Elma Napier's Estate'
Postcolonial Text: 'The Geography of Tea', 'Not the Country I
  Was Born In'

Latitude, Longitude (Kelsay Books, 2021)

Caribbean Quarterly: 'Ode to Sappho', 'Walcott's Lament'
MOKO: 'Sun Spots'
PREE: 'Straw', 'Secret Society'
The Punch Magazine: 'Pink Wall Clock', 'Sun Prayers', 'Island
  Wave'
Sargasso: 'Jigsaw', 'House of Mirrors', 'Winter Survival'
SurVision: 'Leonara's Landscape', 'The Poem is Here'

Pink Typewriter (Kelsay Books, 2023)

Calabash.com: 'Allamanda', 'Maidenhead'
Bermuda Biennial: 'Fontana Degli Artisti', 'London Taxi
  Windshield Wipers'
The Bermudian Magazine: 'Underwater Flight'
The Caribbean Writer: 'Coronavirus Moon', 'Pink Typewriter'
Illuminations: 'Small White World', 'Fair'
Jamaica Observer: 'Home, Home', 'Home'
Journal of Postcolonial Writing: 'Gombey Fire', 'Flag'
MOKO: 'Landfall'
Sargasso: 'Sea Wise', 'Tribe Roads'

9 781915 606488